Patterson Elementary School
3731 Lawrence Drive
Naperville, IL 60564

Nature's Children

PARAKEETS

by

Robert Hirschfeld

Grolier Educational

FACTS IN BRIEF

Classification of Canaries

Class: *Aves* (Birds)
Order: *Passeriformes* (Perching birds)
Family: *Fringillidae*
Genus: *Serinus*
Species: *Serinus canarius*

World distribution: Native to the Canary Islands. Found the world over as pets.

Habitat: Caged birds, kept in homes and other places.

Distinctive Physical Characteristics: Colorful bodies. Fine singing voices.

Habits: Known for their singing. Timid and nervous in disposition.

Diet: Domestic birds live on commercial seed with additional commercial treats.

Classification of Parakeets

Class: *Aves* (Birds)
Order: *Psittaciformes* (Long-pointed tails)
Family: *Psittacidae*
Genus: *Melopsittacus*
Species: *Melopsittacus undulatus*

World distribution: Grasslands and sparsely wooded areas of central and south Australia.

Habitat: Wild birds live in forested areas. Domestic birds live in cages.

Distinctive Physical Characteristics: Colorful bodies. Blue band at top of beak marks male birds. Brownish band marks females.

Habits: Can be trained to do tricks and to talk.

Diet: Domestic birds live on seed. Enjoy leafy green vegetables and commercial treats.

Library of Congress Cataloging-in-Publication Data

Hirschfeld, Robert, 1942-
    Parakeets / Robert Hirschfeld.
        p.   cm. — (Nature's children)
    Includes index.
    Summary: Describes the physical characteristics, behavior,
    habitats, diet, and domestic care of parakeets.
    ISBN 0-7172-9070-0 (hardbound)
    1. Budgerigar—Juvenile literature. 2. Canaries—Juvenile
literature.   [1. Parakeets.]   I. Title. II. Series.
SF473.B8H57 1997
636.6'865—dc21

97-5982
CIP
AC

This library reinforced edition was published in 1997 exclusively by:

 Grolier Educational
Sherman Turnpike, Danbury, Connecticut 06816

Set ISBN 0-7172-7661-9
Parakeets ISBN 0-7172-9070-0

Contents

Humans have always been fascinated by birds, and people have been keeping birds as pets for thousands of years. In ancient Greece, for example, parrots were highly prized, while the Romans brought birds from Africa and housed them in expensive, elegant cages.

Today birds of many varieties and sizes are kept as pets, the most common being the ever-popular parakeets and canaries. Inexpensive to buy and easy to care for, these brilliantly colored birds make excellent companions as they perch willingly on their owners' fingers, shoulders, or heads.

Each bird has its own appeal. Canaries can fill a room with lovely songs, while parakeets often are trained to do tricks or to speak human words. Owners who are willing to take the time and trouble can even breed these birds, providing themselves with fascinating new pets.

A parakeet makes a colorful addition to any home.

Where Do They Come From?

The modern parakeet is a member of the parrot family that originated in Australia, where huge flocks of these colorful birds can still be seen in the wild. This origin is evident in the nickname these birds have in many other parts of the world—"budgies," from budgerigar, which is similar to a native Australian word for "good food."

Canaries are named for the Canary Islands, off the coast of the African country of Morocco, where Portuguese explorers first noticed the birds back in the 1400s.

Unlike their domestic cousins, wild canaries are a rather uninteresting greenish-yellow color. Nor are their songs especially pretty. Over the years, however, breeders have developed many striking varieties of canaries. Some were bred for vivid colors; others, for their singing voices.

Today's domestic canaries are more colorful than their wild relatives.

Which Bird Is for You?

Which to buy—a parakeet or a canary— depends on several things. First of all, someone who wants to fill a home with song should get a canary. Parakeets chirp and chatter quite happily, but they never really burst into song.

Anyone interested in training a bird, however, should choose a parakeet. Parakeets, unlike canaries, can be taught to do tricks—to play with toys, to roll over, to pretend to be "dead." With a little more time and effort they can even learn to talk.

Future owners should think, too, about whether they wish to breed their pets. Parakeets, for example, are a much better choice for someone who wants the excitement of watching baby birds hatch and grow.

People also should know that parakeets need company. They are, in fact, so social that their health can suffer if they are alone too much. People who can have only one bird—or who cannot spend much time with their feathery pets—definitely should choose a canary.

With many colors to choose from, picking the right parakeet can be quite a problem.

Setting Up a Cage

An appropriate cage is an important part of keeping a bird healthy and happy. But just how does someone go about setting up the right kind of cage for a parakeet or a canary?

To begin with, the cage should be big enough to let the bird hop around or even make short flights. In addition, it should be made out of a rustproof material, such as stainless steel, and there should be a slide-out bottom to make cleanup easier. Wooden perches are also a must.

The cage should always be placed well off the ground so birds needn't worry about predators. (Predators are animals that live by feeding on other animals.) It also should be kept out of any drafts, which are a major cause of illness in birds. The cage should also have a fitted cover to keep out the drafts at night.

Most birds enjoy toys, and the cage should always have several. But there still should be enough room for the bird to fly around a bit. Toys can be switched now and then to provide variety.

A bird's cage should be chosen carefully.

More Cage-y Things to Know

Parakeet and canary cages must be kept clean. To make the job easier, the bottom of the cage is lined with paper, which can be thrown out and replaced in seconds. Paper towels, waxed paper, and even plastic wrap all make good liners. Newspaper is not appropriate because the ink on the pages can be poisonous to birds.

The floor liner is changed weekly; the metal bottom of the cage gets a quick cleaning at the same time. Wooden perches are cleaned, too.

The cage also needs three cups—one for seed, one for water, and one for grit, which is a special kind of gravel that helps birds digest their food. These cups must be kept full at all times.

Parakeets enjoy their cage homes.

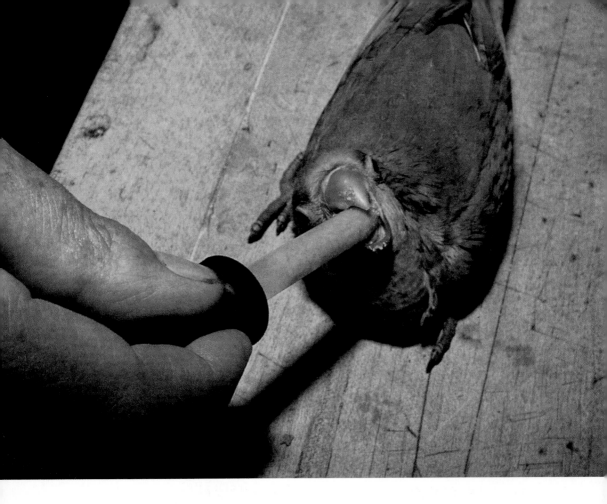

Eyedroppers are a handy tool for giving birds small doses of medicine.

Eating and Drinking

Parakeets and canaries eat special seeds that are sold in pet stores. Each day owners should remove the empty shells and add fresh seeds. The birds' drinking water must also be changed on a daily basis.

In addition, birds need a steady supply of fresh greens. Lettuce, parsley, or spinach can be fastened to the wires of the cage with a clothespin. Greens must be carefully washed in order to remove any dirt, germs, or chemicals left over from fertilizers and pesticides.

Birds enjoy fruit, too, so a piece of apple can be wedged between the cage wires. Because greens and fruit tend to spoil quite quickly, they should not be left out for more than a day.

Table scraps or greasy foods should be avoided. Instead, owners can give their birds any of the special bird treats sold in pet stores. Too many treats, however, are definitely not a good thing. They can make birds fat—or even ill.

True Grit . . . and Cuttlebones

Because birds have no teeth, they cannot "chew" food. Instead, they swallow their food whole. The food goes into a part of the bird's stomach called the gizzard, where it is ground up and digested with the help of grit.

Found in most pet stores, grit is sprinkled on the floor of the cage and kept in a special cup. The grit in the cup is changed every few days; each time the cage is cleaned, fresh grit is sprinkled on the floor.

A cuttlebone is also necessary for any parakeet or canary. (A cuttlebone is the inner shell of a cuttlefish, a relative of the squid.)

Exactly why is a cuttlebone important? A bird's beak never stops growing; but as the bird pecks at the cuttlebone, its beak gets worn down. In this way the cuttlebone acts as a file, keeping the beak from becoming overgrown. Cuttlebones also add calcium to the bird's diet.

Once they are trained, parakeets can be let loose for exercise and fun.

Keeping Healthy

Regular—and sometimes even emergency—health care is necessary for just about every pet, and birds are no exception. Although parakeets and canaries do not need regular checkups, they do need an occasional visit to a veterinarian. As a result, every bird owner needs to know the location of a nearby vet who treats birds.

In addition, birds' claws grow continually. In the wild claws are worn down as birds climb and scratch on rough surfaces. Domestic birds, of course, do not do much of this, so their claws must be clipped. But clipping can cause bleeding if it is not done just right. As a result, most owners choose to have it done by a vet.

Beyond this bird owners monitor, or watch, their pets for any signs of illness. If a bird loses its appetite, has no interest in playing, or seems sleepy most of the time, there is a good chance it is ill. A visit to the vet is probably in order.

Home Sweet Home

Birds—especially canaries—need time to get used to a new home. Owners should do their best to help them adjust as quickly as possible.

A pet bird usually comes home in a small box. To get the bird out of the box, the lid is opened and that end is placed against the open cage door. Most birds simply hop right in. If this does not happen, the bird can be gently lifted out of the box and put into the cage.

Parakeet cages can be placed just about anywhere. Owners simply have to be careful to avoid direct heat or drafts.

Canaries, however, are nervous by nature and need time to adjust to any big changes in their lives. When a canary first comes home, for example, it should be placed in a quiet room. For a few days loud noises or sudden movements that might frighten the new bird should be avoided. In time the bird will become comfortable in its new surroundings and can then be moved to a more social location.

Breeding parakeets is fairly easy—and a lot of fun.

Choosing the Right Parakeet

Parakeets are highly social and love to play and interact with one another. To many people watching this socializing is one of the great joys of owning parakeets.

All this, however, must be put aside by anyone who seriously wants to train a parakeet. The fact is that if a parakeet is going to be trained to do tricks or to talk, it must live alone. If it is with other parakeets, the bird will be too interested in the other birds to pay much attention to its owner.

Young birds—three months old or less—are easier to train than more mature birds. In addition, although females, or hens, are capable of speaking, males, or cocks, are better and faster learners.

Once they are grown, baby parakeets must be trained, just as their parents were.

Home Healthcare for Parakeets

Like all pets, parakeets sometimes develop health problems. Luckily, however, owners can learn to recognize and take care of many of these ailments on their own.

Watery eyes, for example, usually mean a cold—probably from a draft. Pet shops sell remedies for this that can be put in the bird's water.

Watery droppings often are a sign of diarrhea. The first thing to do for this is to avoid feeding the bird greens for a few days. If the diarrhea does not stop, medicine is available in pet shops.

If there are only a few droppings in the cage, the bird may be constipated. Small doses of a mild laxative usually will help. Long-term cures, however, generally involve changes in diet.

A parakeet that scratches and pecks its feathers may be infested with tiny parasites called mites or lice. Pet shops sell liquids and sprays to treat this. If a parakeet starts pulling out its feathers, however, the bird may just be bored. New toys often can put an end to this.

Finger Training Parakeets

As soon as a parakeet is used to its new cage, it can be finger trained. This process begins with the owner slowly moving a long pencil in and out of the cage, several times a day. All the while he or she calms the bird with gentle words and sounds.

Once the bird seems comfortable with this, the owner gently strokes its breast with the pencil. In time the bird will climb up and perch on the pencil.

Next the owner substitutes a finger for the pencil. After a few days the bird should perch on the person's finger. Once the bird readily hops onto a finger, it can slowly be removed from the cage. Eventually the bird will move around to the owner's other hand, shoulder, or even head.

Trained parakeets will quickly return to their owners' fingers.

Talk It Up

Most parakeets are natural mimics and will learn to repeat human speech if they hear the same words often enough. It is important to remember, though, that birds do not understand the words they repeat. They are only making sounds, not conversation.

A parakeet will not learn to speak unless it is alone in its cage. It also is best to have only one trainer so the bird gets used to that person's way of speaking. Training begins with a word or simple phrase such as "Hello " or "pretty bird." It should be repeated—clearly and loudly enough for the bird to hear—many times each day. Once the bird masters its first word or two, it will learn new ones more quickly.

An owner who doesn't have enough time to repeat words over and over again can use an audio tape. Prerecorded tapes are available at pet stores, or the owner can even make a tape of his or her own voice.

A few hours of training can lead to a talking parakeet!

Breeding: Getting Started

Parakeets are fairly simple to breed and raise. There are, however, a few things future breeders need to know.

First of all, breeders will need both a hen (a female bird) and a cock (a male). Male parakeets have a blue cere, or bridge, at the top of their beaks; on females the cere is brown. A nest box, which can be found at almost any pet store, should be purchased as well. The nest box fits onto the doorway of the cage. It has a round opening for the birds, a panel that opens to show what is happening inside, and a bowl-shaped area in which eggs are laid.

The floor of the nest box should be covered with wood shavings, dry grass, or anything else soft enough to cushion the delicate eggs. Grass or straw should be scattered around the floor of the cage; the birds will use this for nest building.

Birds that are breeding need plenty of greens. They also need mineral supplements and extra calcium. This calcium strengthens the eggshells as well as the bones of the baby birds.

Breeding pairs need time to become friendly.

Bringing Up Babies

When a female parakeet lays an egg, she rolls it into the middle of the nesting box and puts it under her breast feathers. She usually lays an egg a day for five days. Parakeet parents take turns sitting on the eggs until hatching time, about 18 days later.

As baby parakeets hatch, the eggshells should be removed from the box so the babies do not hurt themselves on the sharp edges. Unhatched eggs should be removed as well.

Newly hatched parakeets are blind and are covered only with some downy, yellow feathers. Their diet consists of partly digested food fed to them by their parents.

Over the first four or five weeks of life, the babies develop quickly. In what seems like no time at all they are ready to leave the nest. Then, as soon as they start to fly and eat seeds on their own, they are ready to be trained.

Canary cages should be big enough to let the birds hop around and fly a bit.

Choosing the Right Canary

One of the strange facts about canaries is that the best singers usually are fairly plain looking, while the brightest, most beautiful birds rarely have first-rate singing voices. As a result, people who buy canaries usually must make a choice between a bird with beautiful feathers and one that makes beautiful music.

The most active singers are males. Interestingly, hens barely sing at all. The best singing birds, by the way, are called rollers and choppers.

With time and effort canaries can be trained to do a few simple tricks. As with parakeets, anyone who wants to train a canary should have just a single bird. But owners need not worry that a lone canary will be unhappy. Canaries are nowhere near as social as parakeets, and they are perfectly content being alone.

Like parakeets, canaries can be trained to sit on owners' fingers.

A Cagey Canary Story

Canaries are very sensitive to temperature—even more sensitive than parakeets—and can become quite ill if exposed to blasts of chilly air. For this reason a canary's cage should be placed away from windows, doorways, and other drafty spots.

Canaries also are extremely nervous about predators. Their cages should never be placed on or near a floor or within reach of wandering cats.

It also is important for canaries to have a room that is dark and fairly quiet at night. (Even in the wild canaries go to sleep at sunset.) Covering the cage at night helps, but still, canaries should never be placed in rooms that will be noisy during the evening and night.

Finally, canaries love to bathe. Once a day a shallow dish of water should be put on the cage floor for them to wet their feathers.

Canaries should be kept out of direct sunlight.

Keeping Canaries Healthy

When it comes to health care, canaries are similar to parakeets and many other birds as well. But there are a few special problems that can arise with pet canaries.

When a canary's eyes turn red and it starts to wheeze while breathing, the bird probably has a cold. (Canaries catch cold easily—more easily than parakeets.) Luckily, treating a canary's cold usually is simply a matter of adding some medicine— available at any pet store—to the bird's water. A bit of honey added to the bird's seed will help too.

Canaries can also have problems with heat stroke. To avoid this, keep the cage out of direct sunlight. If a bird does seem to be suffering from the heat, however, it can be revived with a quick spray of water or a gentle rub with a damp, cool cloth.

Canary breeders always have beautiful new birds to enjoy.

Going into Training

Canaries cannot be trained to talk or do the complicated tricks that parakeets can do. But a little basic training is possible. This not only is fun, but it can allow owners to let their birds loose for flight and exercise.

Finger training a canary takes at least 15 or 20 minutes a day. The owner begins by slowly approaching the cage, talking or whistling softly until the bird no longer seems nervous. As with a parakeet, the owner then slowly moves a stick or a finger into the cage, stroking the canary's breast until the bird perches.

When a bird is willing to perch on its owner's finger, it can be removed from the cage to continue its training. The best place for this is a small room with few things the bird can bump into or hide behind. In time, the canary will fly freely and then return to perch on its owner's hand or shoulder.

Canaries are not just yellow; they also come in unusual colors.

Getting the Parents Acquainted

Breeding season for canaries is in March. This means that anyone who wants to breed canaries needs to have both a male and a female bird by December. This gives the birds time to get used to each other before they breed.

Unlike parakeets, canaries need a special breeding cage. This cage is divided in half by two movable barriers, one wire and one solid. The birds also need a nest, which can be bought at a pet shop. It is lined with soft cloth and hung midway up the side of the cage.

In February the hen is put in one half of the breeding cage and the cock in the other, with both the wire and solid barriers in place. At this time the hen starts eating a special breeding food, which is available in pet stores.

After five days the solid barrier is removed so the birds can see each other. Several days later the owner hears a mating call—a high, piping whistle. The wire barrier is then removed, and the breeding cage is placed in a quiet room.

Breeders can create birds with special colors or traits.

Egg Time

When mating calls begin, it is time to put nesting material into the cage—bits of string, cotton, dry grass, or even dog hair. The owner must also buy six dummy, or imitation, eggs from a pet store.

After the birds finish their nest, the hen lays an egg every day or two until there are three to six eggs. Each new egg is carefully removed from the nest with a spoon, and in its place goes a dummy egg. (Using a spoon helps keep the eggs from breaking.)

The real eggs are moved to a bed of oatmeal, sand, or cotton and carefully turned once a day. When all the eggs are laid, the dummy eggs are removed and the real eggs are returned to the nest. Then, because male birds sometimes will harm newly hatched babies, the owner puts the wire barrier back in the cage and moves the cock to the other side.

Why use dummy eggs? This is done so that all the eggs will hatch at one time. If the eggs hatched over several days, the parents would have to work a lot harder to care for the babies.

Caring for Baby Canaries

As they hatch, baby canaries seem helpless, almost unable to get out of their shells. But an owner should never try to help them hatch. The sad truth is that a chick that cannot break out of an egg by itself is not likely to survive on its own.

Once the chicks hatch, the mother is given special breeding food. Apples and milk-soaked bread are usually mixed in with it. After eating this food and partially digesting it, the mother will feed it to her babies.

About six days after the babies hatch, the mother begins sleeping on a perch instead of in the nest. At this point the barrier is removed from the cage.

When the chicks are 18 days old, the owner starts giving them their own "baby food." (The food is made by soaking seeds for 24 hours and drying them on a paper towel for a day.) At the age of six weeks the chicks can crack the shells of the seeds for themselves.

Getting Along with Other Pets

Anyone who already has other pets and plans to get a bird should keep these few thoughts in mind.

No matter how lovable and cuddly a cat or dog may be to its owner, to a bird it will be a very scary creature. At the same time, a cat, no matter how well behaved, will always think of a pet bird as a tasty meal. So even if a cat has never shown any interest in a parakeet or canary before, it still should never be left alone in the same room with a bird.

Dogs are less likely to attack birds, but birds can still be frightened by them. When a bird is badly scared, it may never fully recover from the experience.

Parakeets make wonderful friends.

Shows and Exhibits

Everyone knows about dog shows and cat shows. But not many people realize that there also are shows for parakeets and canaries.

Most pet-shop owners and vets have information about how to get in touch with parakeet and canary clubs. These clubs organize and run local shows at which bird owners can present their pets and compete for prizes.

Anyone who wants to learn more about showing birds should attend one or two exhibitions. Who knows? This could be the beginning of a fascinating new hobby. At the very least there probably will be some delightful new birds to see and hear!

Words to Know

Budgerigar Name used for parakeets in many parts of the world; similar to native Australian word for "good food"

"Budgie" Nickname for parakeet.

Cere The bridge across the top of an adult parakeet's beak; blue on cocks, brown on hens.

Chopper A type of canary bred as a singer.

Cock A male parakeet or canary.

Cuttlebone The inner shell of the cuttlefish; gnawed by birds to keep their beaks from overgrowing.

Gizzard The part of a bird's stomach where it uses grit to grind up its food.

Grit Fine gravel birds need to digest food.

Hen A female canary or parakeet.

Millet A kind of seed eaten off the stem by canaries and parakeets.

Roller A type of canary bred as a singer.

INDEX

Cover Photo: SuperStock, Inc.
Photo Credits: Betts Anderson (Unicorn Stock Photos), pages 13, 17, 20, 22; Norvia Behling (Behling & Johnson Photography), pages 4, 7, 11, 29, 31, 33, 35, 39, 41, 45; Fred D. Jordan (Unicorn Stock Photos), page 26; Ted Rose (Unicorn Stock Photos), page 36; Charles E. Schmidt (Unicorn Stock Photos), page 25; SuperStock, Inc., page 8; Wildlife Conservation Society, page 14.